MY POEMS/ MY LIFE

MY POEMS/ MY LIFE

R. RICHARD CRAIG JR.

Library of Congress Control Number:		2019911758
ISBN:	Hardcover	978-1-7960-5208-4
	Softcover	978-1-7960-5207-7
	eBook	978-1-7960-5206-0

Print information available on the last page.

Rev. date: 08/13/2019

To order additional copies of this book, contact:
Xlibris
1-888-795-4274
www.Xlibris.com
Orders@Xlibris.com
800730

CONTENTS

RELIGIOUS POEMS

LOVE POEMS

NONSENSE POEMS

THIS BOOK IS DEDICATED TO

Mrs. Winifred Craig Henderson (My Mother)
Linda Craig Jones (My Sister)
Rosaleita Yolanda Craig (My daughter)

POEMS

YOU

There is nothing you can't do,
Nothing you can't be,
For you are all and all is in thee.
You are the best of two world,
The very essence of man,
Full of compassion and Love,
With the need to understand-YOU.
For you are all and all is in thee.
For you have the Power to decide, for yourself,
What you desire to be.
For you are all.

EQUALITY

For just one word, EQUALITY, many men have fought and died,
Fought the Germans and the Japanese, just to keep that one word alive,
And through the many wars we had, somehow, it has survived,
But, now when we need it most, it seems like it has died,
America how great thou art,
But, still thou art so small,
For a country cannot be truly great until there is EQUALITY for ALL.

WHO-WHAT AM I

I am a Man, both Black and Proud, A Man-
Regardless of What anyone else may say, I am a Man,
And like any other Man, there are several things I want,
Several things I need, several things I desire to have,
Among all my wants, needs, and desires,
There is one thing, that to me, in order to be a Man,
A REAL MAN, I must have,
And that one thing is RESPECT,
As other men need Respect,
So as a Man-do I
I ask you, is RESPECT too much for me, as a Man
To ask for, to demand of you?

MOTHER

For very soon we'll be gone,
But, Mother's love will still go on,
They taught us to walk,
They taught us to pray,
Taught us to thank God for a brand new day,
Just one day out of the year,
We honor our Mothers, whom we love dear,
Who took care of us with loving care,
And helped us conquer our doubts and fears,
So at this time I would like to say-
"GOD BLESS YOU MOTHER ON MOTHERS DAY."

MY WORLD

My world is so very small
That the universe has no time for it,
My world is but a dream
Filled with memories of happy things,
For my world is a perfect world,
In my world there are no wars,
No disease, no hunger,
No pain, just love, a world of love,
My world, my world, my own little world,
What will happen to you when I grow up?
What will happen to me when you are no more,
And I must go out into this cruel, cruel world of reality?

LIFE

Life is short,
So, go out and enjoy every moment of it.
Dare the impossible,
Search for the unknown,
Look, search, conquer, and then forget it,
For life is short, it's over before it's begun.
Life, what is this thing called life,
Is it existing from one day to another in your own self-made hell,
Or is it being a pawn in someone's gigantic chess game
Your move, my move,
Your move, my move
You're dead, I'm dead
Checkmate,
The game is over,
And so is life.

MAN

I am Man
Present since the beginning of time
I am all
And yet I am nothing
I am the warmth of the day
And the lovliness of the night
I am the moon which glows so bright in the sky,
And invites others to follow me.
I was born-created
And life was blown into my mouth
I grew up, matured, turned old and died
And with death, returned to the dust I came from
And I left lonliness behind me
I need companionship
I need love
I need to be needed.
For I am all
But without love, the love of a good woman
I am nothing
I am Man
Weak, Conceited, Scared
I Need!

BIGOTRY

From the depth of man's mind I've come
Conceived in jealousy
Born in hypocrisy
Raised in misery and mistrust
I am here
For as long as there is man
There shall I be, also
For as long as there are wars
People shall know my name
For as long as there is hunger
People shall feel my hands
For wherever there is hatred
You shall see my face
Many organizations do bear my mark
And many wars have been started thanks to me
I have caused brothers to kill their brothers
And mothers to deny their own
I am always present
For without me, what would man do
If man could not hate his fellow man
Then what is left for man to become
For I have helped man create the atomic bomb
And started many wars across the sea
Helped man to kill his fellow man

And pollute the air and seas
For I am bigotry
Disgusting, corrupt, evil
I'll always be around

WHEN LOVE IS GONE

Love is a very dear and precious thing
So, if you are one of the very lucky ones to have found love
Then hold love, keep it, never let love go
For when love has gone, all has gone
Your prayers, your hopes, your dreams
When love has gone, all has gone
Your life is an empty thing
When love has gone the sorrow comes
And problems one by one
When your lover's gone
There's no one there to help you solve each one
For your love has turned and gone away
And there's no one there beside you
Your love has turned and gone away
And sorrow is around you
Love, oh love, where have you gone
Shall you return to me one day
Love, oh love, where are you now
My problems are here to stay
I found love, lost love, and now I'm alone
In this world of emptiness, I'm here alone
All alone in this, my misery
Love
What an easy word to say and yet the meaning great

To love someone with all your heart
And love them until it aches
To lose love is a terrible thing
For one as young as I
For now my love has gone away
And now I want to die
Love is gone and I am here
And sorrow is here, too
Now, I ask you
What is left
What can I do
When love is gone

THE GIFT OF LIFE

I was blessed with life
And yet I wonder why was I given this great honor
Why couldn't I have stayed where I was
Be it in the warmth or be it in the cold
Or be it in the pitch of dark
Why was I given life
Why am I here
Mother, why did you borne me
I am now the same as I was yesterday
And yet I am different
I see and yet I do not see
I talk and yet no one hears me
I pray and yet my prayers are not answered
Why am I here
I was born and so I have life
I am alive and so I must breathe
I breathe so I can stay alive
But still I am dying
Why must I die
Why must I live and then why must I die
Today I am, yesterday I was, tomorrow what will I become
A great man once said, "I came, I saw, I conquered"
I'm here, I see, but I have nothing to conquer
There's no water for me to drink

No wine for me to taste
I'm here but no one cares
I speak but no one hears
I look but I no see

TIME

Time has gone, time has passed me by
Like so many others, I must lay my tired body down and sleep
For I have done all I could in my short life
I've been happy and I've been sad
I've experienced love and lost
Recaptured what I had and lost it once again
Now I'm tired
Time has run out for me, life has passed me by
And it's time for me to rest
Now it's time for me to think about all the things I've done
And of all the things I could have done in my life, but didn't
It's time for me to rest
Time for me to rest and think of all the mistakes I've made
And how, if only I was given another chance
How I could undo the things I've done
Time
If only I were given a few seconds more
I would apologize to you for all I have done to you
But the saddest thing about that is
That you may wonder what did I do
You would say I hadn't done anything to you, for you or against you
That is what I want to undo
I want to help you, my fellow man
Time has passed me by, life has passed me by

I-I have gone
When I go, will there be anyone to care for me
When it's my time to leave, will there be someone to survive me
To say I have lived
Is there anyone who really care for me
Will there be anyone to shed one tear for me
Will I just be buried in a plot of land,
With a stone above my head.
When I'm dead,
Five years after I'm buried, will there be anyone to say,
Craig, Craig had lived,
Craig, Craig had done well,
Or will someone just say,
Craig-who's Craig?
Or will someone else, when they are asked about Craig,
Will they say
Craig- SH*T.

BORN WITHOUT LOVE

I was born in a world where there was no love
I was born in a world where there was no love
I am, I was created, I was born, and so I have life
And yet, what is life without love
What is life without love
I need love
I need to have someone near me
I need to have someone caring about me
I need my identity, I need warmth, and consideration
But above all I must have love
I was born in a world without love
I was born in a world without love
I need love
Like a bird needs its freedom to fly
And that same bird has a song to sing
So love is my song and life is my flight
And I'm lonely, and I'm afraid
Because I am and yet I am not
I need love to live

JUBILEE

One hundred years have come and gone
And still we are not free
One hundred and sixteen years have come and gone
And still we're in Jubilee[1]
Although the chains have been removed from our hands
And chains removed from our feet
We are still not free
For our minds, our minds are still in chains
And without those chains removed we can never be truly free
Free-to think for ourselves
Free-to determine our own destiny
Free-to question the past, our past
But most importantly, to be free enough to have faith in today
And a real hope in our tomorrow
One hundred years have come and gone
And still we are not free
One hundred and seventeen years have come and gone
And still you are in slavery

---

1   Jubilee–The period of transition from slave to free

LIFE

Life is short,
So, go out and enjoy every moment of it.
Dare the impossible,
Search for the unknown,
Look, search, conquer, and then forget it,
For life is short, it's over before it's begun.
Life, what is this thing called life,
Is it existing from one day to another in your own self-made hell,
Or is it being a pawn in someone's gigantic chess game
Your move, my move,
Your move, my move
You're dead, I'm dead
Checkmate,
The game is over,
And so is life.

THE CHAIR

I was stranded here in N.Y.C.
And a help line, sent me to G.P.C^{2*}.
There we Blacks and Whites and Hispanics there,
And they were all held captured by their GOD-the chair.
They took their GOD to breakfast, lunch and dinner too,
And after the wake- up meeting in their chair they were glued.
From 9am-4pm no music could they play,
But after 4pm-the residents had their way.
Curse this, curse that's all you heard them say,
As the disrespected themselves all night and all day.
Men and women used the same JOHN at the same time,
Living, existing, like this for many was fine.
As long as they had their GOD-the chair.

---

2 * GPC-grand central station's emergency housing

C.S.I. IN MARYLAND

C.S.I. in Maryland is a joke,
It's the enemy of OLD FOLKS.
Life is more than LOW RENT indeed,
Life is creating new goals and fulling our needs.
Maryland's mgt and some Liaisons have no respect,
As they control their building and creating a mess.
Changing their bi-laws and house rules at will,
If you don't like what's happening here LEAVE.
This isn't only what they say, but it is what they believe,
Because this is business and not about the Seniors need.
C.S.I. in Maryland-Great concept- POOR LEADERSHIP.

By- R. Richard CRAIG, Jr.

MY VIEWS ON POLITICS

A CHANGE HAS COME

A Change has come to America,
A change we did not see,
A Change has come to America,
A change to extreme Liberalism and Negativity.
A change has come to America,
As Liberals blame G.W. when anything goes wrong,
A change has come to America,
As we sell our country out for a song.
A change has come to America,
High unemployment on its way,
A change has come to America,
Socialism in here today.
A change has come to America,
As NObama apologies for our past,
A change as come to America,
As we kiss our enemies ASS.
For change, Nobama change has come- Do you like it?

SORRY TED

Lying, crying Ted,
He's so sad,
I would not be surprise-
If he still wet the bed,
A poor excuse for a Christian for me.
He's very prideful and arrogant and sickening you see,
A crybaby who don't keep his word,
Disliked by fellow senators and as for me I concurred.
Go away lying Ted- continue to cry,
Your action and pledge is just a lie.
Sorry Ted-Good bye

I NO LONGER RECOGNIZE AMERICA

I no longer recognize America- My country, My land
I no longer recognize America-Our Republic for which I stand,
I no longer recognize America-The country where I was born,
I no longer recognize America-or it's strange Values that I now moan,
America you we so GREAT, But thanks to NOBAMA, you are so small,
For a country can- not be truly Great- until we honor our citizens rights
and equally follow our laws.
U.S. CITIZENS FIRST.

R. Richard Craig, Jr. 7/19

CRAZY UNCLE JOE

Crazy Uncle Joe,
A third run- OH NO,
How sad are those DAMOCRATS indeed,
As those socialist ignore America's need.
Climates change is a joke,
Especially for RICH FOLKS.
Medicare for all is the same,
It will not effect the rich or political game.
Welcome back crazy Uncle Joe,
You will lose again as we knows

THE SQUAD

The GARBAGE Squad, that's what you are-
3 born near (in America), and 1 born in FAR (Somalia).
All are American Citizens what a shame,
As they play the socialist, Racist Damocrat game.
They are NOT very smart as you can tell,
If they don't repent they will go to HELL.

By- R. Richard Craig, Jr. 7/19

RELIGIOUS POEMS

TO THE GLORY AND
HONOR OF GOD

TO HIM

To Him,
Let's love him all of our days,
To Him,
Let's give him all honor, all praise
To Him,
The creator of the Heavens and Earth,
To Him,
Through Christ's death we are freed from sin's curse,
To Him
In the Heavens and Earth forever he reigns,
To Him,
Blessed be GOD's holy name,
To GOD give him all glory and all praise,
Give all glory and all praise to GOD.

To: Mother

GOD'S GLORY

The wind that blows cool air upon the saved and unsaved,
Screams GOD's Glory.
The sun that warms us by day and the moon and all the stars
that guides us by night,
Screams GOD's Glory.
The trees that grows towards the heavens and gives us shade
during those sunny days,
Screams GOD's Glory.
The flowers which blossoms and when we see them-we smile,
Screams GOD's Glory.
The water that refreshers us when we thrust,
Screams GOD's Glory.
That MOTHER who loves and take's care of her children,
Who gently teaches them to walk, talk and pray,
Screams GOD's Glory.
For everything that was created and exist Past, Present, future
and forever more-
Screams of the Glory of GOD

I THANK THEE

I thank thee, O Lord, for seeing me fit,
To live in this world with all of this,
Where people sin and kill one another,
I thank thee, O Lord, for giving me a mother,
Another thing I thank thee for-
Is for giving me a home and food,
For giving me clothes to wear to church,
For giving my mother the strength to give me birth,

I THANK THEE

ETERNAL LIFE

Peter, Paul, and Bartholamew, all disciples of Christ,
He told them the wonders of heaven and of eternal life,
If ye seek eternal life you must do those things that are right,
For an example:

       Go to church everyday, don't forget at night to pray,
       Honor your Mother, your Father too,
       For this is a commandment that God sent unto you,
       And then one day we all shall meet, Up in heaven,
       Where there is peace,
       Peace from hate, trouble, and temptation,
       Home with God we shall start a new nation,
       A brand new nation free of sin,
       A godly nation that will never end,
       With God, our Father, the Supreme and most High,
       We shall never grow old, sick, or die,
       We shall not think of these earthly things,
       But, we shall be home with God, our Father, our King.

THE DEVIL

Do you know about the Devil and all his evil works?
How he tried to conquer heaven and he fell upon this Earth,
Do you know about the Devil and all the things he did,
How he told King Herod to cut off John the Baptist's head,
He even tried to tempt our Savior, Jesus Christ,
Whose purpose on this Earth was to give to us His life,
If you could see the Devil, I can imagine what he would say,
He would brag about the things he did back in the biblical days,
He would tell you about the Garden, and Adam's wife Eve,
Who ate of the apple from God's forbidden tree,
He would tell you about Cain, Adam's oldest son,
Who killed his brother, Abel, and found no place to run,
He would tell you about Sodom and Gomorrah and all the things the
people did,
Who broke God's commandments just like the Devil did,
But, God destroyed those cities with fire and brimstone,
And Satan failed once more to build himself a kingdom above God's
mighty own.

THE JOURNEY

Another day has come along,
Another day for me to face on this my journey,
The road is both big and wide,
And I have no one by my side, to confront me,
Another day, another way, another reason I have to say,
That I am here and alive on this, God's land, God's land,
This, my journey, is long and rough-
And there's so many obstacles in my way,
But, nevertheless, I can't look back, I can't look around,
I can't stop, can't rest,
I must look straight, walk straight, with my head up high,
Looking not at the Earth, but, at God's sky, God's sky,
For this isn't just a journey, my journey, but, it's God's journey,
For I know my goal is somewhere straight ahead,
It's not a place for me to stop and rest and then return,
For I know that once I reach my goal, I'll never return,
For It's a place with warmth and love,
And you can find it up above, in a place called--Heaven,
My journey, my destiny is to Heaven.

I SHALL STRIVE

I shall strive to do those things that's right,
I shall strive to please God in his almighty sight,
I shall strive to live up to the things I say,
Because I want to see God after Judgement Day,
I shall strive to be obedient in every sense of the word,
For I want to be a lamb of God in His almighty herd,
All the things I learned in the Church of God,
I shall hide it in my soul,
Whether something is good or shall it be bad, these things shall I know,
So, when I make an account of all my sins, I shall strive to have none,
So, that God may say, "Well done, well done, Richard, my fateful son."

ARE YOU TRYING

Are you trying with all your might,
To do the things you know that's right?
Or are you doing everything right-right one day,
And on the other days curse, drink, and act so gay?
Just remember this before sin you do,
That Jesus Christ, He's watching you,
He's writing down the things you do, whether it's good or bad,
He's writing down everything you do, and everything you said,
For Jesus Christ, He's right up there looking, writing, watching you,
So, this is my advice to you and you, that in your faith each one be true,
Because Jesus Christ is right up there looking, writing; He's watching you.

MY PRAYER

Oh, Lord of lords, God of gods,
Hear this my request, for only thou can grant them unto me,
For thou has the wisdom and the power to do this,
For thou knows all things, including my thoughts,
my wishes and all my desires,
And with this knowledge, Dear God,
I am sure that thou knows that my request is true,
Grant me simply four things:
Faith, Hope, Love, and Happiness-
Give me faith in today, hope in tomorrow, and eternal love,
For I know, Dear God, that without these first three things
that I could never hope to gain the fourth and most important
thing-happiness,
Oh, hear me, Dear God, hear me.

CHILDREN'S VERSES

After dinner I go to bed,
and dream of angels around my head,
I pray to God that I may see,
One more day to worship thee.

The sun is down,
The sky is black,
And now it's time to take a nap,
But, before you take a nap, you pray,
That the Lord may spare you another day.

LOVE POEMS

A LOVER'S PRAYER

Oh, look upon us Oh ye gods,
And smile upon me and my love who is so far away,
Hear all our prayers and grant them unto us no matter what they may be,
Grant us love, true love, not just a love that is here today and is gone tomorrow,
But, give us a love that will grow and ripen while we are apart,
And will bloom and blossom when we are together,
Oh, hear me Oh ye gods, hear me.

BARBARA JEAN

I love that girl Barbara Jean,
I love the way that she can sing,
Summer, Fall, Winter, Spring,
I Love that girl-"EVERYTHING".

- And Robert Coates

M.J.B.

I love that girl M.J.B.
The way she is so sweet to me,
I'll swim the oceans,
I'll swim the seas,
Just to have her talk to me,
Just to see her make a smile,
Makes my life on Earth worth- while,
So whatever you say, whatever you do,
Please remember M.J.B. that I LOVE YOU

I DESIRE TO MEET YOU

BY R. CRAIG 11/21/97

MY DAYS ARE SO LONG AND SO EMPTY INDEED-
SO I DESIRE TO MEET YOU.
YOU MAYBE THAT SPECIAL ONE, WHO I TRULY NEED-
SO I DESIRE TO MEET YOU.
PLEASE CONTACT ME, AND LET US SEE,
IF I'LL FOR YOU AND IF YOU'RE FOR ME-
FOR I DESIRE TO MEET YOU.....

ARE YOU?

BY. R. CRAIG 11/21/97

ARE YOU THAT SPECIAL SOMEONE, THAT I'VE BEEN LOOKING FOR?
ARE YOU THAT SPECIAL SOMEONE TO WORSHIP AND ADORE?
ARE YOU THAT SPECIAL SOMEONE, WHO CAN MAKE MY LIFE COMPLETE?
ARE YOU THAT SPECIAL SOMEONE, I'VE ALWAYS LONGED TO MEET?

ARE YOU?

LET ME, LET US

I know your worth,
Let us dream new dreams,
Let us listen to each other's cry,
And dry each other's tears.
Let us cradle life's pain,
With us there's no shame,
Let us free all our fears,
And let us give each other cheer.
Let me, Let us-Be there.

NONSENSE POEMS

THE BOSTON TEA PARTY

In the year 17 hundred and 73
The British decided to place a tax on tea,
The Colonists were upset as upset as could be,
And so they decided to buy no tea,
They met one night when the moon was bright,
And they decided they would fight,
They went to the port where the ship did lie,
And they spoke to the Captain with an awful cry,
They urged the Governor to send back the tea,
But, when he refused they became mad as could be,
Disguished as Indians from head to toe,
They attacked the ship and the rest you know-
About the Boston Tea Party.

THE ALAMO

One day they fought there,
Lived there, died there,
For me and you and our country, too,
At the Alamo.
The Mexicans caught the Texans by surprise,
They retreated to the Alamo and there they died-
At the Alamo.

A SPARROW

On a roof cold and narrow,
Falls my little falling sparrow,
Down, Down into the world,
that sparrow is a girl.

WASHINGTON

Over the Oceans, Over the Seas,
There's a country just for me,
At the capital in Washington, D.C.
There's a man- That's me.

CPSIA information can be obtained
at www.ICGtesting.com
Printed in the USA
BVHW071008190819
556215BV00007B/147/P